The FIRST BOOK of

AMERICAN EXPANSION

Final boundaries of the United States of America, prior to the addition of Alaska and Hawaii.

The FIRST BOOK of

AMERICAN EXPANSION

by Wyatt Blassingame

Illustrations by Fred Sweney

FRANKLIN WATTS, INC.
845 Third Avenue, New York, New York 10022

To Miss Kathi
And to any new states
she may see
come into the Union

FOURTH EDITION

SBN 531-00457-1

Library of Congress Catalog Card Number: 65-11741

© Copyright 1965 by Franklin Watts, Inc.

Printed in the United States of America

Contents

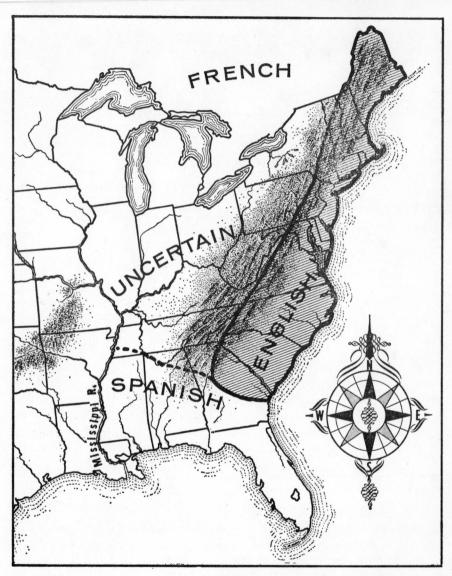

Original French, Spanish, and English claims in North America.

a) Christopher Columbus   *b) John Cabot*

Dividing the New World

The First Boundary Line

POPE ALEXANDER VI never saw the New World. He believed that the land Christopher Columbus had discovered when he sailed southwest across the Atlantic in 1492 was really a part of India. In 1493, however, the Pope drew the New World's first boundary line.

Columbus, employed by the King and Queen of Spain, had been looking for a short route to India. At the same time, Portugal had been sending explorers southeast along the coast of Africa looking for the same thing. Since both Spain and Portugal had been looking for the East, the Pope said the new land should be divided between the two countries. He drew a line down the blank spaces of his map, roughly three hundred and fifty miles west of the Cape Verde Islands. Everything west and south of that line he gave to Spain, and everything east and south of it to Portugal. This, he said, included not only what Columbus had already discovered, but everything that ever would be discovered.

I

There was one big trouble with this first boundary line—no nation, except Spain and Portugal, was willing to agree with it. In other countries men asked, somewhat bitterly, if the Pope had a deed to the new land from Father Adam. If he did not, how was it his to give away? Soon explorers from most of the countries in Europe were crossing the Atlantic to see what they could discover, and to claim their discoveries for their own kings.

Fish, Furs, and Discoveries

COLUMBUS himself never saw any part of what is now the United States. His voyages took him through the Bahama Islands, the West Indies, and on to the coast of South America. Most of the early Portuguese and Spanish explorers followed this same route. In 1497, however, five years after Columbus made his voyage to the New World, an Italian navigator and explorer named John Cabot (Giovanni Caboto) reached the mainland of North America. Cabot, employed by King Henry VII of England, sailed across the North Atlantic and came to Cape Breton Island, off the coast of present-day Canada. The next year he returned to North America and this time followed the coast southward. He himself was not sure how far he sailed. It may have been to the Chesapeake Bay area, or it may have been all the way to Florida. However far it was, it was far enough to give England a claim to vast amounts of land in the New World.

Cabot may not have been the first man of his time to reach the coast of North America. Fishermen do not always tell where they find the best fishing, and it is certain that within a few years after Cabot's voyage there were English, French, and Portuguese fishing boats working off the coast of Newfoundland every summer. On the shore, they established temporary settlements where they could dry their fish so that it would not spoil

Jacques Cartier

on the long voyage back to Europe. Some of these fishermen, particularly the French, began to trade with the Indians for furs. Others went past Newfoundland to Nova Scotia for still more furs.

In 1534, a Frenchman, Jacques Cartier, sailed up the St. Lawrence estuary "until land could be seen on either side." The next year he went up the river until his way was blocked by the rapids at Lachine. This country, Cartier decided, was too cold for permanent settlement, but there were wonderful furs to be bought cheaply from the Indians.

The Spanish, meanwhile, had established towns on Santo Domingo, Puerto Rico, and Cuba, as well as in Mexico and South America. In all these places Spanish civilization was flourishing and Spanish officials were growing rich, while the great mainland to the north remained a wilderness.

It was not until 1565 that the Spanish established St. Augustine, the first permanent city in what is now the United States. The first permanent English colony was Jamestown, in Virginia, founded in 1607. A year later, in Canada, the French established their first permanent colony, Quebec.

And so the first real boundaries in North America were drawn, with the Spanish settled in the south, the English in the middle, and the French in the north.

The Spanish Flag is planted on Florida soil.

A Confusion of Claims

THE TROUBLE with these boundaries was that they overlapped. When the Spanish claimed Florida they also claimed everything north and west of it. What that everything might be, nobody knew. The English claim, set forth in 1606, was to all the land between the thirty-fourth and forty-fifth parallels, or from just south of the present city of Wilmington, North Carolina, to what is now the northernmost part of Maine's coastline. Unfortunately, nobody could agree on the western limits of this claim. Some colonies claimed land all the way to the Pacific, with no idea of how much land that included. Already French trappers and priests were moving along the St. Lawrence River and the Great Lakes, claiming the inland country for France. Much of this was south of the forty-fifth parallel.

4

To add to the confusion, the Dutch claimed land along the Hudson and Delaware rivers. The Swedes also claimed land along the Delaware. Eventually, the Dutch would drive out the Swedes, and the English would drive out the Dutch, but the great struggle that would set the first legal limits of the United States would be between Spain in the south, England in the middle, and France in the north. Already its outlines were clear.

From 1608 on, for approximately a hundred and fifty years, the English settlements spread gradually along the Atlantic coast from Maine to Georgia. The French moved west along the Great Lakes, then south along the Mississippi River. These French were chiefly trappers and traders who lived with the Indians. They established no large colonies like those the English were developing along the Atlantic. In the south, the Spanish established only a few small settlements in an area that is now divided into Florida, Georgia, and Texas.

A World at War

DURING this century of conflicting claims and expanding boundaries in the New World, Spain, France, and England were engaged in an almost endless series of wars for world power. Sides changed constantly. Sometimes England and Spain fought against France; sometimes Spain and France fought against England. At other times each nation was for itself. These wars were reflected in America. The settlers not only fought the Indians for new land, they also fought one another. As a result, boundary lines changed continuously. In May, 1719, France captured Pensacola from Florida, lost it back to Spain in August, and recaptured it later the same year. Three years later France lost it again. Along the Canadian border some of the land changed hands almost as rapidly.

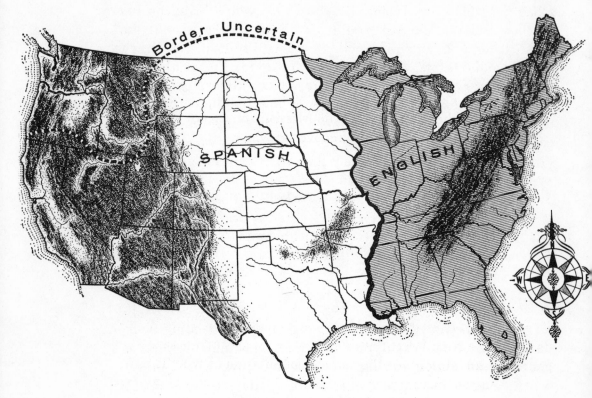

1763. Spanish and English territorial claims.

Finally, in 1763, at the end of what was called the Seven Years' War in Europe, and the French and Indian War in America, there was peace—at least for a while. Under the Treaty of Paris (1763) France surrendered Canada to England, along with all her claims to land south of Canada and east of the Mississippi River, except for the city of New Orleans. This city, along with all French claims to land west of the Mississippi and south of Canada, went to Spain. Spain, in turn, surrendered Florida and all her lands east of the Mississippi, except for New Orleans, to England, in order to recover Havana.

New Borders for the New World

FOLLOWING the French and Indian War, new borders were drawn in North America. France no longer had any possessions on the mainland. England owned Canada and everything east of the Mississippi. Spain received everything west of the Mississippi and south of Canada, with the exception of a vaguely defined area beyond the Rocky Mountains that was claimed by Russia, Spain, and England. West of the Mississippi, the southern border of Canada was still uncertain, but it did not matter very much at that time. The country was inhabited mostly by Indians. Almost all of the colonial population of what is now the United States was centered along the Atlantic coast and along the Gulf between Pensacola and New Orleans.

More important than the land beyond the Rocky Mountains at that time was a new border drawn by King George III through his own possessions in October, 1763. This was called the Proclamation Line. It ran south from Canada along the crest of the Appalachian Mountains, separating the rivers that flowed toward the Mississippi from those that flowed toward the Atlantic. At its southern end, where it reached what had been Spanish Florida, it swung eastward to the ocean. No Atlantic colony, the

King announced, could extend west of this Proclamation Line, no matter how much land a colony had previously claimed. Nor could any settlers move into the territory. The purpose of the line was to separate the colonists from the Indians, and so maintain peace. It would help keep the peace, the King believed, by separating the English from the Spanish colonies on the Mississippi, and would also help protect the fur trade, which would suffer if agriculturists moved into the Mississippi Valley.

There was still another reason for the line, which George III did not mention publicly. It was intended to keep settlers from moving into the unclaimed area and grabbing land for themselves. If no one could lay claim to the land beyond the Appalachians without the King's permission, then the King could sell the land bit by bit to land companies whenever he thought best.

The Great Migration

THE PROCLAMATION of 1763 had the same weakness as the papal bull issued by Alexander VI in 1493: the people who disagreed with it paid no attention to it. East of the mountains land was getting more and more scarce, and the colonies more and more crowded. In the rich valleys watered by the Ohio and other rivers flowing into it, there was ample land to be had for the taking. Of course, there were Indians beyond the mountains, but the men who lived along the western edge of the colonies had been fighting Indians for years anyway.

Soon the pioneers were pouring westward. Some went by land, driving their cows and horses and pigs in front of them. Their wagons were often piled so high with households goods that even the women and children had to walk. Some settlers floated down

8

A Conestoga Wagon

the Ohio River on rafts loaded with everything they owned, including their livestock. They made their way up tributary rivers —the Miami, the Kentucky, the Wabash, and the Cumberland. Where the land was fertile they stopped; there they built cabins and planted crops. It made no difference to them that the King claimed the land for himself. There were not enough English soldiers in the wilderness to turn them back. Within two years after the proclamation, more than five thousand settlers had crossed the mountains. Within another three years the number had grown to thirty thousand.

Most of these pioneers came from the colonies of Virginia and Pennsylvania. They did not know it, but they were helping to shape the first map of the as-yet-unborn United States.

1783. The first boundaries of the United States.

The Treaty of Paris

THE AMERICAN REVOLUTION began in 1775, twelve years after George III established the Proclamation Line. The settlers who had poured across the mountains were as American as the men at Bunker Hill, and they, too, took a part in the War for Independence. They wanted the land they occupied to be part of the new United States.

The first boundaries of these United States were drawn at the Treaty of Paris (also known as the Treaty of Versailles) in 1783. Not only the American colonies, but also France and Spain, had been at war with England. The demands of all three countries, as well as those of the United States had to be considered.

Although Spain owned vast areas west of the Mississippi, these areas were populated mostly by Indians. Spain did not want the aggressive, land-hungry Americans on her border. The western boundary of the United States, Spain insisted, should be kept well east of the Mississippi. England also wanted the United States confined to a narrow strip along the coast, because she was determined to hold on to the land between the mountains and the Mississippi.

France, too, wanted the United States kept small. Although she no longer had possessions in America, she had been an ally of the Americans against the British and believed that if the new country were kept small and weak it would still be dependent on her.

And so, on the point of size, three great nations were aligned against the one new nation still weak from its struggle for independence. The simple fact remained, however, that the land between the mountains and the Mississippi was in the possession of Americans. They would not give it up without fighting, and nobody wanted another war.

Finally the borders of the new country were drawn. The Anglo-French wars of the seventeenth and eighteenth centuries had more or less established the St. Croix River as the boundary between Maine (which was then still part of Massachusetts) and the Canadian province of New Brunswick. This river was now accepted as the border between Canada and the United States. From the source of the St. Croix, the boundary ran due north to a range of hills, called the Highlands, that separated streams flowing toward the Atlantic from those flowing toward the St. Lawrence River. The boundary followed the crest of the Highlands to the Connecticut River and continued down the river to the forty-fifth parallel (the northern limit of the land claimed by England in 1606) and along the forty-fifth parallel to the St. Lawrence. From the St. Lawrence the border followed the middle of various rivers and lakes, almost exactly as it does today, to the southwestern corner of the Lake of the Woods. From there it ran due west to the Red River of the North at the point where Minnesota, North Dakota, and Canada now touch.

From this westermost point of the new United States, the boundary followed the Mississippi south to the thirty-first parallel. This is the line that today separates Florida from Alabama. The line ran east along this parallel to the Chattahoochee River, down that to the Flint River, and straight east from there to the St. Marys River. It then followed the St. Marys to the Atlantic. This southeastern border had been more or less established by previous wars as the boundary between Florida and Georgia.

Florida, like Canada, had remained loyal to England during the Revolution, but now, as a result of the war between England and Spain, Florida was returned to Spain to whom it had belonged in 1763.

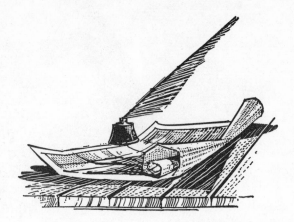

The "Red-Line Map."

Thus the first limits of the United States were established. In the northeast the line was very much as it is today. In the south it was Spanish Florida. On the west it was the Mississippi River.

Border Trouble

THE FIRST trouble over the new boundaries occurred in an area where very little change has taken place in all the years since its creation, and which today is considered the world's most peaceful border—that between the United States and Canada.

The line between Maine and Canada was supposed to follow the top of the hills, separating the streams that flowed toward the Atlantic from those that flowed toward the St. Lawrence. This was an easy way to set a boundary line, but the people who lived in the area found it difficult to know exactly where the line was. Settlers in Maine grabbed land that Canada claimed, and settlers from Canada grabbed land that Maine claimed. The controversy went on and on, becoming more and more heated. Several times the United States came close to war over the problem.

13

Benjamin Franklin

It would have helped if there had been an accurate map. While the Treaty of Paris was being negotiated, Benjamin Franklin, one of the American officials in Paris, had drawn a "strong red line" on a map to show the American border. He had given this map to the French minister, but it had disappeared. During all the years that the United States and Canada argued over the border, nobody could find the "Red-Line Map," as it was called.

Finally, in 1842, the United States and Great Britain signed the Webster-Ashburton Treaty, which settled several disputes. The chief result was the determination of the U.S.-Canadian border where it is today. Then, in 1932, almost a hundred and fifty years after it had disappeared, a copy of the Red-Line Map was found—not in France, but in Spain. It was an accurate copy, made at the time Franklin drew the original. This map substantiated the American claim, and might have altered the outcome of the Webster-Ashburton negotiations in the United States' favor if it had been available then. However, at the time of treaty's signing, its terms were satisfactory to both nations.

Napoleon Bonaparte

The Louisiana Purchase

A Strange Treaty

NAPOLEON BONAPARTE was a young revolutionary and military genius who rose to be First Consul of France. In 1800 Thomas Jefferson was elected President of the United States. At almost the same time Napoleon was making himself dictator of France. No two men could have differed more. Napoleon believed that people could not govern themselves and had no right to do so. Jefferson believed passionately in democracy and said that the best government was the one that governed least. Napoleon gloried in war, while Jefferson worked hard to keep his country at peace. These two men, nevertheless, working together, doubled the size of the United States. They also started the country on what would later be called its "manifest destiny," a phrase which suggested the inevitability of the continued territorial expansion of the country until it controlled the whole North American continent from coast to coast.

15

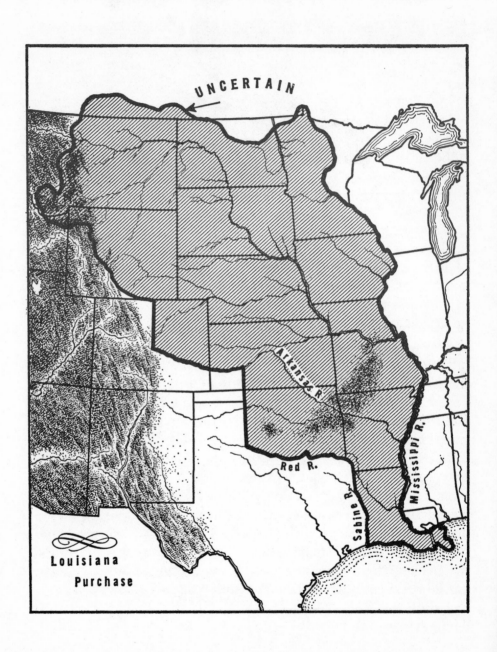

The story is a strange one—perhaps one of the strangest in the history of the United States—for Napoleon sold territory without knowing what he was selling, and without any right to sell it, while Jefferson bought territory without knowing what he was buying, and believing that he had no right to buy it.

As has so often happened in the history of the United States, the destiny of the young republic was closely linked with events in faraway Europe. Even before Jefferson became President, Napoleon's armies were sweeping across Europe, conquering country after country. Like many another dictator, however, Napoleon wanted more and more. An empire in Europe no longer satisfied him. He wanted to restore the empire France had once owned in the heart of America. At the conferences leading to the signing of the Treaty of San Ildefonso, in the year 1800, Napoleon persuaded Spain to return the territory west of the Mississippi that France had lost to her thirty-seven years before. In exchange, Napoleon placed the son-in-law of the Spanish king on the newly created throne of Etruria.

There were two odd things about this Treaty of Ildefonso, and both of them would affect the history of the United States. First of all, the treaty was not put into effect immediately. It was kept secret, and for awhile no one in the United States government knew that the land on the country's western border had changed hands. Second, nobody, not even Spain and France, knew exactly what this territory included. It was all called Louisiana. In the north it bordered on English-owned Canada, in the southeast it bordered on Spanish Florida, and in the southwest it touched Spanish-owned Mexico. The problem would have been simple if anyone had known exactly where these borders lay, but no one did know. Only one thing was certain—the Louisiana Territory included New Orleans and the surrounding area on both sides of the Mississippi River. Whoever controlled this territory controlled the city and the river.

17

Jefferson Makes a Decision

WHEN the Spanish-French dealings were finally made public in 1802, Jefferson became deeply worried. It was one thing to have Spain in control of New Orleans; to have France in control of the city was something else. Spain was too weak to develop or fortify her American holdings. She had, moreover, granted the United States the "right of deposit" at New Orleans. This meant that the American frontiersmen who lived between the Appalachian Mountains and the Mississippi River could send their goods downstream to the port where, without charge, they could transfer them to oceangoing ships which would carry them to markets in the East and in Europe. Because of the difficulty of transporting goods across the almost roadless mountains to Atlantic ports, the water route out of New Orleans was absolutely necessary to the survival of the settlers living west of the Appalachians. With the French in control of New Orleans, there was no assurance that the Americans would be allowed free access to this important port.

Jefferson rightly suspected that Napoleon planned to build an empire along the frontier of the still-weak United States. He also suspected that France and England were about to go to war. The United States had a navy, but it was too small to keep the French out of New Orleans. But with the help of the English navy it might succeed.

Jefferson had never really liked or trusted the English. On the other hand, he had grown deeply fond of the French people during his service as American ambassador to France. Jefferson's first loyalty, however, was to his own people, and so when he began to suspect Napoleon's ambitions in the United States, he wrote a letter to Robert R. Livingston, American minister at Paris. In this letter he declared, "There is on the globe one single

Thomas Jefferson

spot, the possessor of which is our natural and habitual enemy. It is New Orleans . . . The day that France takes New Orleans . . . from that moment we must marry ourselves to the British fleet and nation."

Jefferson did not want war, but he could see only one chance of avoiding it. He instructed Livingston to try to buy the Isle of Orleans, on which New Orleans stood, from Napoleon. Not knowing that the Florida territory still belonged to Spain, he instructed Livingston to buy that as well. If Napoleon would not sell New Orleans, he said, perhaps he would sell another commercial site on the Mississippi, or at least guarantee the permanent establishment of the right of deposit at New Orleans. If Napoleon refused to sell anything, then Livingston was to go to England and make plans for the United States to join the British if they went to war against France.

After writing to Livingston, Jefferson called in his friend James Monroe. He explained the situation and told Monroe to go to France to assist Livingston with the negotiations. At this time Jefferson had absolutely no thought of buying the Louisiana Territory. It was too vast, too empty. It did not even occur to him that Napoleon might be willing to sell it. Moreover, he did not think that he, as President, had any real right to buy any foreign territory. Believing in a strict interpretation of the Constitution, he was certain that the President and the federal government had no powers except those specifically given them. Nowhere did the Constitution say that a President could buy new land. It was only the desperate need to keep the Mississippi open that made Jefferson buy any territory at all.

Napoleon Breaks a Promise

IN 1800, when he signed the Treaty of San Ildefonso, Napoleon had thought that his country and England would be at peace for some time. In order to build his American empire he would have to send ships back and forth across the ocean, and only England had a navy large enough to prevent this. Peace with England was important to Napoleon's long-range plans.

James Monroe

By the end of 1802 things had changed. Napoleon now saw no hope of avoiding war with England. If war came, England would cut France off from her American possessions. Either England or the United States could easily capture the settlement at New Orleans, and with it lay claim to the whole Louisiana Territory. Any way he looked at it, Napoleon could see no chance of building an American empire until he had defeated England.

Napoleon at that time was also faced with another problem—money. It would take a great deal of money to fight England. As was his habit, he made up his mind quickly. In the Treaty of San Ildefonso he had promised Spain never to turn Louisiana over to another country, but promises meant nothing to him. Even before James Monroe arrived in France, Napoleon had sent a message to Robert Livingston. Instead of buying just New Orleans, he asked, why not buy the whole Louisiana Territory?

Livingston was flabbergasted. He had no authority to buy a territory that size—a territory as large as the whole United States at that time. Monroe had no such authority either, but both men agreed that the purchase of Louisiana would mean too much to the future of the United States to be turned down.

There was little time to decide. If Livingston sent a message to Jefferson, he might not receive an answer for months. The message, or the answer, might even be captured by foreign ships. In the meanwhile, Napoleon might change his mind about selling.

Both men knew that if they signed to buy the territory, the contract would not be binding on the United States without Jefferson's consent. As President, he would have to make the final decision.

The two men argued briefly with a representative of Napoleon over the price, then signed the treaty on April 30, 1803. The

United States was to pay 60,000,000 francs, or about $11,250,000, for the Louisiana Territory, and to assume certain French debts to American citizens. These amounted to 20,000,000 francs, or $3,750,000, which meant that the United States was really agreeing to pay approximately $15,000,000 for the territory. Later, with interest and other charges added, the total price came to $27,267,622.

Jefferson recognized instantly the great importance of this vast new territory. He had been interested in the land beyond the Mississippi for many years. Even before he had any idea that the United States could buy it, he had made plans to have it explored. He was convinced, however, that the purchase was unconstitutional. Under the terms of the sale, the citizens of Louisiana must be given all the rights, advantages, and immunities of citizens of the United States. This meant that a new state would have to be formed and taken into the Union. Jefferson did not believe that he alone had the power to agree to the purchase, but he realized what it could mean to the country.

Jefferson's advisers reminded him that he, as President, had the power to make treaties with foreign nations. Under this power, they said, he could make a treaty with France to buy Louisiana. Still doubtful of its legality, Jefferson signed the treaty, then asked that the Constitution be amended to give him the power to do what he had already done.

Neither Congress nor the public worried as much about the Constitution as Jefferson did. The Senate ratified the treaty, but the Constitution was not changed. From that time on it would be generally accepted that, when acting for the welfare of the nation, the federal government would have "implied powers" beyond those specifically named in the Constitution.

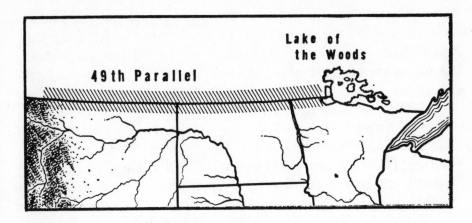

Boundaries in Dispute Again

Now that it had purchased the Louisiana Territory, what had the United States actually obtained? Jefferson himself insisted that in the northwest Louisiana reached all the way to Oregon. England and Spain refused to agree with this. And nobody really knew the exact location of the line between Louisiana and Canada on the north.

The argument between the United States and England went on for fifteen years. During this time the two countries fought the War of 1812, which had nothing to do with boundary disputes, but did grow out of Napoleon's war with England. Only after the War of 1812 ended was the old argument over the extent of the Louisiana Purchase at least partially settled with the signing of the Convention of 1818. By this agreement the border between the United States and England was fixed along the forty-ninth parallel, just where it is today, running from the Lake of the Woods to the crest of the Rocky Mountains. The land beyond the Rockies was left open to occupation by subjects of both countries for a period of ten years.

In the southeast there was still another argument. Before France lost all her American possessions, the area along the Gulf Coast between the Mississippi and the Perdido rivers had been considered part of Louisiana. Under the British it had been part of Florida. In 1803 it belonged to Spain, but the United States claimed it as part of the Louisiana Purchase because it had once been part of Louisiana.

There was a similar dispute in the southwest. Here the border between French Louisiana and Spanish-owned Mexico had never been clearly drawn. In actual practice, it was about where the border between Louisiana and Texas is today, but France had made vague claims to land all the way to the Rio Grande. The United States, therefore, claimed this land as part of Louisiana. These arguments with Spain would not be settled for sixteen years.

Gradually the borders of the Louisiana Purchase came to be defined as the Mississippi River on the east, the Gulf of Mexico from the Mississippi to the Sabine River on the south, then north along the Sabine River to latitude 32 degrees north, and then due north to the Red River. Along the Red River the line ran to longitude 100 degrees west, then straight north to the Arkansas River, and along this all the way to the river's source. From there it ran due north to latitude 42 degrees north, and from there along the crest of the Rockies to the Canadian border.

It was an area of approximately one million square miles. From this territory would be created the states of Louisiana, Missouri, Arkansas, Iowa, Minnesota, North and South Dakota, Nebraska, and Oklahoma, along with parts of Kansas, Colorado, Wyoming, and Montana.

All this land cost the United States only about four cents an acre.

Juan Ponce de León

The Story of the Floridas

Who Owned Florida?

WHEN JUAN PONCE DE LEÓN claimed Florida for Spain in
1513 he believed it to be an island, and he claimed the whole
thing, however big it might be. In the early sixteenth century
Spanish Florida actually had neither a northern nor a western
boundary because no one knew what lay where in those direc-
tions.

By the early eighteenth century, however, Florida had shrunk
to very much the same size and shape as it is at present. English settlers had taken the land north of the St. Marys River (now
the eastern border between Florida and Georgia) and French-
men were west of the Perdido River. In 1763 Florida became
an English colony. Under England the name Florida was given
to all the land along the Gulf westward to the Mississippi. Here
it went north to approximately the thirty-second latitude—
about where Vicksburg, Mississippi, is now. The northern
border of Florida ran due east across what is now Mississippi and

25

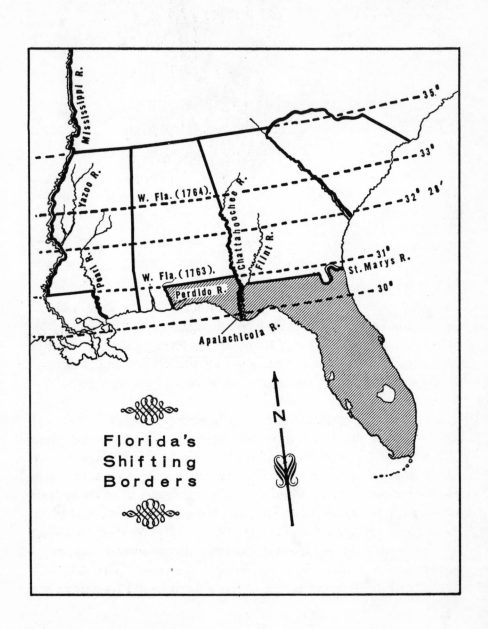

Mississippi R.

35°

33°

Yazoo R.

W. Fla. (1764).

32° 28'

Chattahoochee R.

Pearl R.

Flint R.

31°

St. Marys R.

W. Fla. (1763).

Perdido R.

30°

Apalachicola R.

N

Florida's
Shifting
Borders

Alabama to the Chattahoochee River. There it turned south to the Flint River, and then east again, much as it does today. But England divided this large colony into two parts—everything east of the Apalachicola River was called East Florida, everything west of the river was called West Florida. Together they were called "the Floridas." This was the cause of much of the confusion that was to follow.

England held the Floridas for only twenty years; then she returned "Florida" to Spain. But was the Florida she returned in 1783 the same size it had been under Spain? Or was it as big as the Floridas had been under England?

There was no easy answer because England had made one treaty with the United States and another with Spain. In the treaty with the United States, which was made first, England said that if Florida was returned to Spain, its northern border would be 31 degrees. This is the same as the present east-to-west border between Florida and Alabama, and about one hundred miles south of where the border had been under England. In the English treaty with Spain this border was left unsettled, and Spain claimed all the land south of 32° 28′, the old border under England.

As a result, a strip of land approximately one hundred miles deep and almost four hundred miles long, stretching all the way across what is now Mississippi and Alabama, was claimed by both Spain and the United States.

With the secret treaty between Spain and France in 1800, the situation began to get really complicated. In this treaty Spain returned Louisiana to France. At one time French Louisiana had included the towns of Biloxi and Mobile and all the land along the Gulf as far east as the Perdido River—all of which England had included in West Florida.

Did the Louisiana that Napoleon got back from Spain include this area? Or, as Spain claimed, did the Louisiana she had ceded lie altogether west of the Mississippi, except for New Orleans?

As long as France made no effort to take over Louisiana from Spain this was not important, but when Napoleon sold the territory to the United States, things changed. Did the United States or Spain now own Biloxi and Mobile and the narrow strip along the Gulf? Which one owned the much bigger strip to the north?

Spain had a few very small forts in the area, but almost no settlers. On the other hand, American frontiersmen, always hungry for land, soon pushed westward into the area from Georgia and the Carolinas. From the Kentucky country they came down the Ohio and Mississippi rivers to settle around what now includes Vicksburg and Natchez, and on the rich farming land to the east. Within a few years the question of who owned the land between 31 degrees and 32° 28′ was finally settled on the basis that Americans possessed it in fact (if not legally), even though Spain still claimed it.

There were also Americans south of the thirty-first-degree line, most of them in the area just east of the Mississippi River.

James Madison

These Americans were a mixed lot. Some of them were honest farmers; others were outlaws who had fled the states to the east. Some were gamblers, speculators looking for a way to get rich quick on a new frontier. Many of them sincerely wanted to be a part of the United States. Many others merely thought they saw a way to get free land.

On the night of September 26, 1810, approximately one hundred of these men attacked the small Spanish fort at Baton Rouge. The fort was half decayed, manned only by a handful of soldiers. There was a brief skirmish. The two Spanish officers were wounded, and their soldiers fled or were captured. With that, all the actual fighting in the West Florida revolution was over.

The American settlers quickly held a convention. They declared themselves to be the independent state of the Republic of West Florida and promptly sent a message to President Madison asking to be annexed by the United States.

Madison issued a proclamation on October 27 announcing United States' possession of West Florida, from the Perdido to the Mississippi. He authorized its military occupation as part of

A Seminole Indian

the Louisiana Purchase. He did not admit that there had ever been any such country as the Republic of West Florida, and the rebel speculators never got the big land grants they had hoped for.

The only part of West Florida that U.S. troops occupied was the area between the Pearl River (now the border between Mississippi and Louisiana) and the Mississippi River, and so, by 1811, the United States once more had a new border.

Meanwhile, in East Florida, conditions were becoming even more confused than in West Florida. Outside of St. Augustine the Spanish made almost no effort to control the country. Seminole Indians roamed at will. Negro slaves in southern Georgia often ran away to join them. The Seminoles themselves sometimes raided Georgia settlements, then fled back into Florida where the settlers could not get them. And as the Georgia frontier became more populated, men looked hungrily at the empty land to the south.

Trouble With Spain

WHEN the United States went to war with England in 1812, President Madison was afraid the British navy might use Mobile as a base, so he ordered it occupied by American troops. The weak Spanish garrison surrendered without a fight, and American soldiers took over all the land west of the Perdido River.

Spain did not actually join England in the War of 1812, but she did allow English agents to work in Florida. These agents urged the Indians to go on the warpath against the Americans. Then, in August, 1814, England landed two hundred marines in Pensacola.

Quickly Andrew Jackson marched an American army southward. The United States was not at war with Spain, but that did not bother General Jackson. He attacked Pensacola, captured it, and held the city until he was sure England could not use it as a base.

Shortly after, the war with England ended, but the trouble over Florida continued. By this time Spain had only a handful of troops in Florida. The land was almost totally without government. Slave ships and pirates came openly to the little town

Andrew Jackson

of Fernandina, just south of the Georgia border. Probably no place in United States history has been more completely lawless than the Florida-Georgia border in the second decade of the nineteenth century.

It was a situation that could not be allowed to continue. In May of 1818 General Andrew Jackson got word that the Seminole Indians who had been on the warpath in Georgia were being sheltered by the Spanish. He wrote a letter to President Monroe stating: "Let it be signified to me . . . that the possession of the Floridas would be desirable . . . and in sixty days it will be accomplished." Just what reply Jackson received is uncertain; in any case, he marched his army into Florida and captured Pensacola for the second time. He removed the Spanish officials by force, and then went home to Tennessee and left the confused situation for the diplomats to settle.

After extensive negotiations, this was achieved by the signing of the Adams-Onís Treaty, in which Spain agreed to renounce all claims to West Florida and cede East Florida to the United States. Spain also gave up its claim to any land west of the Rocky Mountains and north of forty-second parallel. In return, the United States gave up its claim that the Louisiana Purchase had included Texas. In addition, the United States agreed to assume Spanish debts to American citizens. These amounted to the $5,000,000-limit the United States set.

Because this treaty dealt with land from the Atlantic to the Pacific, it is sometimes called the Transcontinental Treaty. Under its provisions, the United States stretched down the Atlantic coast from Canada to Key West, for the first time in its history. Beyond the Mississippi, however, the United States was bordered by Spanish-owned Texas and by the uncertain limits of the Louisiana and Oregon territories. There was still more trouble ahead.

Stephen Austin

The Story of Texas

Moses and Stephen Austin

THE ADAMS-ONÍS TREATY of 1819 was also supposed to set the boundaries of the Louisiana Purchase and to draw a line separating the Spanish provinces of Texas and New Mexico from United States territory. The Spanish government, however, was centered in Mexico City, where it was no more able to settle and defend these remote northern areas than it had been able to settle and defend Florida. From time to time soldiers of fortune (called *filibusters*) led tiny private armies into the almost empty country and claimed it for themselves, only to be chased out eventually by Spanish troops. Then the troops would return to Mexico City and another band of filibusters would move into Texas.

These were the conditions when a fifty-nine-year-old man named Moses Austin mounted his horse somewhere near the village of St. Louis and rode south. He rode for more than eight hundred miles, most of the way through Indian country, to the town of Bexar, now San Antonio, which was the capital of Spanish-owned Texas. There he called on the governor of New Spain.

Austin believed that Spain was anxious to have the empty lands in Texas developed, and so he proposed that he be given a contract to bring in three hundred American families. He promised to choose his families carefully, selecting only good, honest men. In return, Austin himself would be given a large grant of land.

The governor refused, then changed his mind. In January, 1821, when Austin rode north again, he carried the Spanish contract with him.

The weather was cold and rainy. Austin's powder became wet, and he could not kill game to eat. Weak from hunger, he contracted a fever. Even so, he kept going until he reached his home in Missouri. A few months later he died.

Now it was Moses' son, Stephen F. Austin, who took over the settlement of Texas. But his first colonists had barely settled on the rich land along the Brazos River when he learned that neither he nor they had any right to the land. Mexico had become independent of Spain. Moses Austin's contract with the Spanish government was no longer any good.

Immediately Stephen Austin set out for Mexico City. It was a twelve-hundred-mile ride, most of it through wilderness country. Before he had gone two hundred miles he was captured by Indians. They did not kill him, but they took his horse, his gun, everything but some money and papers he had hidden in his boots, and turned him loose. They expected him to starve, but

35

he managed to catch a wild horse and rode it bareback into Monterrey. There he got another horse and a saddle and rode on to Mexico City.

Stephen Austin got an even better contract with the new Mexican government than his father had with Spain. Now he could bring in six hundred families rather than three hundred. In fact, the Mexican government soon granted similiar contracts to a number of other persons. These persons who obtained contracts to settle colonists in Texas were called *empresarios* (managers of enterprises). Mexico was so generous with the land it gave to the *empresarios* that a man willing both to farm and raise cattle could get as much as ninety-nine squares miles! For this he was supposed to pay, some day, approximately $1.11 for each square mile. In the meanwhile he did not even have to pay taxes, and under Mexican law his land could not be taken from him, no matter what kind of debts he owed.

The Mexican government did this to attract settlers who would become Mexican citizens. Under the contract, settlers were required to taken an oath of allegiance to Mexico and to become Catholics if they were not already of the faith. But only a few of the settlers, rushing to grab the vast, rich land, took this seriously.

Many of these Americans liked living under the Mexican government. They had more land than they knew what to do with, and the central government, far off in Mexico City, paid little attention to them, which meant that they were really left to govern themselves.

Conflict With Mexico

As AMERICANS continued to pour into Texas, things began to change. Most of the colonists came from the southern United

States, and many of them brought slaves with them. Mexico was opposed to slavery, but allowed slaves to be brought in for a while.

There were several points of conflict. The Americans resented being required to join the Catholic Church. They objected to the fact that under Mexican law there was no trial by jury. Sometimes they found the titles to land on which they had settled disputed by Mexican authorities. On the other hand, the Mexican government saw a part of its country being taken over by Americans who paid little attention to its laws. They realized that Texas was rapidly becoming more American than Mexican.

In 1830 Mexico passed a law prohibiting slavery and the further settlement of Texas by United States citizens, but the colonists kept coming. By 1835 there were about 35,000 Americans in Texas—and less than 4,000 Mexicans.

ALAMO

Alarmed, Mexico began to send troops into the area. This increased the resentment of the Texans, who began to talk more and more about independence.

For a long time Stephen Austin tried to keep the colonists loyal to Mexico, but at last he realized this was impossible. "War," he said finally, "is our only recourse." On March 2, 1836, Texas declared itself independent.

At about this time Santa Anna, the Mexican dictator, was leading an army into Texas. With more than 3,000 troops he attacked the Texan force of about 187 men at the Alamo, killing them to the last man. Another Texan force was defeated at Goliad. It looked as if the independence of Texas would be brief indeed.

Then abruptly the tide turned. On April 21, 1836, a Texan army under General Sam Houston went into battle with the cry, "Remember the Alamo!" and defeated the Mexican army under Santa Anna. Santa Anna himself was captured during this Battle of San Jacinto, and the remnants of his army fled back to Mexico.

This ended the immediate fighting. For all practical purposes Texas was now an independent country. Without opposition, Texans established their own government, adopted a constitution, and elected Sam Houston their first president. In this same election some six thousand Texans voted in favor of annexation by the United States; only ninety-three voted against it.

Texas Joins the Union

TEN YEARS would pass before Texas would become a part of the Union. Although Mexico made no immediate attempt to reconquer Texas, the Mexican government refused to admit its independence. In Washington the Mexican ambassador made it clear that if the United States agreed to annex Texas, Mexico would consider it an act of war.

At that time Andrew Jackson was President of the United States. He wanted Texas. He had been opposed to the Adams-Onís Treaty of 1819, by which the United States released its claim to Texas as part of the Louisiana Purchase, but 1836 was an election year. Annexation of Texas might well mean war, and many people did not want war. To start a war might mean the defeat of Jackson's party in the coming election.

With Jackson's cooperation the Senate voted to recognize Texas as an independent nation, but the Senators did not vote to accept it as part of the Union.

Jackson's Democratic Party won the election, and Martin Van Buren became President. Like Jackson, Van Buren wanted Texas to become part of the United States. By now, however, many persons, particularly in the northern part of the nation, were violently opposed to the annexation of Texas. It was a slave-holding country, and if it was admitted to the Union it would be another slave state. Already the quarrel that would one day lead to the Civil War was taking shape. It was this quarrel, as well as fear of war with Mexico, that continued to block the admission of Texas to the Union.

Meanwhile, Texas was having serious troubles as an independent country. Its population was made up of scattered farms and small settlements. It lived under the threat of a major war with Mexico. Now and then Mexican cavalry troops made swift raids into the country to destroy ranches and small settlements.

The Texan government had neither the money nor the people to support a real army.

Under these conditions Texas turned to Great Britian, and Britain was glad to help. Texas produced a vast amount of cotton that was needed in the English mills and provided a duty-free market for British manufactured goods. Also, England saw an independent Texas as a possible rival to the United States and as a means of blocking the young nation's growth.

This was the situation in the early 1840's. The United States in its brief history had already fought two wars with England, and it wanted to keep English influence out of Texas.

There was also another powerful influence at work on American public opinion. Already pioneers were moving westward to the Oregon Territory. Wagon trains were skirting Texas to trade with the Mexicans in Sante Fe. All over the country people talked of moving west, and of America's "manifest destiny" to expand from coast to coast. As a result, the annexation of Texas became an important issue in the Presidential election of 1844. James K. Polk and his Democratic Party were in favor of annexation. Henry Clay and the Whig Party hedged.

Polk won the election. Immediately Congress, without even waiting for Polk to take office, voted to invite Texas into the Union. On July 4, 1845, a Texas convention approved the annexation. Texas became the twenty-eighth state in the Union on December 29.

But where exactly did its borders and the new borders of the United States lie? According to Texans, the state stretched all the way to the Rio Grande. According to Mexico, the southern border of Texas had always been the Nueces River, which meets the Gulf of Mexico where the city of Corpus Christi is today. And anyway, the Mexicans said, Texas still belonged to Mexico, no matter where its borders lay.

Sir Francis Drake

"Fifty-four Forty or Fight!"

Russia Claims Part of the New World

SIR FRANCIS DRAKE, a red-bearded English buccaneer, was probably the first white man ever to see what later would be called the Oregon Territory. In 1579, he sailed the *Golden Hind* through the storm-swept waters below Cape Horn and turned north. Along the west coast of South America he raided Spanish ships and settlements, taking the gold and jewels the Spanish had stolen from the natives. Then he continued north, searching for the mythical water passage between the North Atlantic and the Pacific.

Just how far he went we do not know, possibly to what is now the southern border of Canada. Eventually he turned west, across the Pacific and back to England.

For almost two hundred years after Drake's voyage the country lay forgotten. Then, about the middle of the eighteenth century, Russian fur hunters began to explore the coast of Alaska. They took home the fabulous sea-otter furs from which fortunes were made. Some of their ships ventured southward along the coast.

Alarmed at the approach of the Russians, the Spanish government in Mexico sent their ships to explore the area. American and British merchants heard of the furs the Russians were bringing home. In 1778, the Englishman James Cook reached what is now Vancouver Island and explored the coast north to Alaska. On May 11, 1792, an American ship captain named Robert Gray discovered a great river, which he named for his ship, the *Columbia*. It was on this discovery—and later on the Adams-Onís Treaty with Spain—that the United States would base much of its claim to what would be called the Oregon Territory.

At the time of Gray's discovery, Russia, England, and Spain also claimed the land, and its boundaries were as uncertain as its ownership. It was south of Russian Alaska, but where exactly did Alaska end? It was north of Spanish California, but where was that? How far east did it go?

Nobody could say for sure.

Settling the Boundaries of the Oregon Territory

IN THE SUMMER of 1793, a bearded Scotsman named Sir Alexander Mackenzie led a small band of trappers over the Canadian Rockies and down to the Pacific—the first white man to cross the tremendous breadth of the North American continent.

Clark

Lewis

In 1803, President Thomas Jefferson appointed Meriwether Lewis, a young captain in the United States Army, to lead an overland expedition in search of a route to the Pacific Ocean. With William Clark, a veteran frontier fighter, Lewis led his expedition down the Columbia River to the Pacific. After them, mostly out of Canada, came a few trappers. In 1811, the American millionaire John Jacob Astor sent trappers to establish a trading post at the mouth of the Columbia. They named it Astoria, for their employer. A few years later, during the War of 1812, this trading post was taken over by Canadian trappers and by the Hudson's Bay Company, for which they worked.

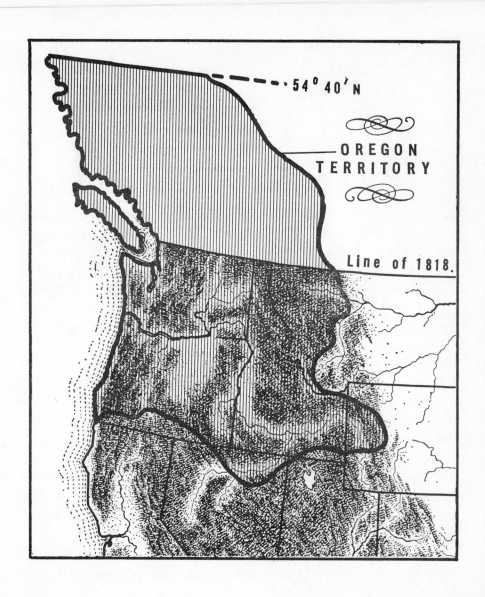

The Treaty of Ghent, which ended the War of 1812, did not try to settle the question of boundaries. This was left to a convention that met in 1818. Here for the first time the northern limit of the Louisiana Purchase and the southern border of Canada were set at the forty-ninth parallel. This line would extend from the Lake of the Woods to the crest of the Rockies. Beyond the top of the Rockies, it was agreed, lay Oregon. Because the convention could not agree on who owned Oregon, it was decided that, for a while anyway, the land would be left open to settlers from both countries. This was called the Joint Occupation Treaty. No attention was paid to the fact that Russia and Spain also had claims to this land.

In the Adams-Onís Treaty signed a year later, Spain relinquished to the United States its claim to any land north of 42 degrees. This set the southern border of the Oregon Territory at 42 degrees and left only three countries—England, Russia, and the United States—to claim it.

Russia was the next to withdraw her claims. In 1824 she signed a treaty with the United States, and a year later a similar one with England. In these Russia gave up her claim to land south of 54° 40′.

And so at last the Oregon Territory had definite borders: from 42 degrees in the south to 54° 40′ in the north; between the Pacific on the west and the crest of the Rocky Mountains on the east. All this territory was claimed by both the United States and England.

In 1827 the two countries renewed the Joint Occupation Treaty, but either country, it was agreed, could cancel the treaty by giving one year's notice.

The land itself remained almost empty, except for Indians. The Hudson's Bay Company had a few small trading posts,

A Fur Trapper

manned by a few trappers. American fur trappers, known as mountain men, roamed the Rockies trapping beaver; sometimes they followed the beaver streams as far west as the Pacific. Back east a few people talked about Oregon, but only a few.

Then several oddly unrelated things happened that, added together, would help shape the map of the United States.

On to Oregon!

IN 1831 four Flathead Indians appeared in St. Louis. They had come, they said, to get Bibles and to learn about the white man's religion. Probably they were not interested in religion as we think of it. To the Indian religion was "medicine." Obviously the white man, with his guns and steel traps, had powerful medicine, and the Indians wanted to learn about it. But their appearance stimulated great interest among church people in the East. Before long missionaries were being sent to Oregon to teach the Indians. The first two white women to cross the Rockies were the wives of missionaries.

46

About this same time the price of beaver pelts began to drop. A mountain man earned barely enough to buy his traps and guns. Some of the trappers began to leave the mountains and to take up farming in the Willamette Valley in Oregon. And back in the East, a man named Hall Jackson Kelley began to travel up and down saying that Oregon, where he had never been, was a paradise for settlers. He advertised for people to go west with him. He got few followers, but he did create talk.

Meanwhile, the missionaries who had gone to Oregon were writing letters home. They were disappointed in their attempts to make Christians of the Indians, but they were impressed by the beauty of the land and the richness of the soil. Their letters were reprinted in the Eastern newspapers.

All at once "Oregon fever" hit the country like an epidemic. Historians have never been able fully to explain it. It was a combination of many things. Partly it was the lure of free land; partly it was the lure of adventure. Some of it was patriotism and the belief that this was the way to secure Oregon for the United States. And partly it was the strange westering drive, almost like the migratory instinct of birds, that for more than two hundred years had kept Americans moving toward new frontiers.

In the winter of 1842-43 a few more people began to advertise that they planned to go to Oregon and wanted people to go with them. Unexpectedly, answers poured in. People formed companies to travel together, and these companies grew and grew. In Kentucky, Tennessee, and Ohio men stopped their work to talk about Oregon. The more they talked the more excited they became. By May of 1843, almost one thousand men, women, and children had gathered in Independence, Missouri, from where the wagon trains would start. By summer more than a thousand wagons were rolling westward over what for ever afterwards would be called the Oregon Trail. In the summer of 1844 even more would follow.

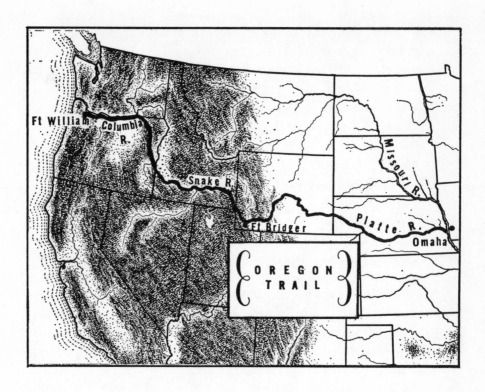

A Compromise and a New Boundary

THE OREGON fever affected politics. At that time James K. Polk was running for President against Henry Clay. Polk's platform called for the annexation of Texas and the occupation of Oregon. In the past there had been talk of dividing the Oregon Territory with England, either along the forty-ninth parallel or along the Columbia River, but now many people wanted to take the land all the way to Alaska. They were even willing to go to war for it. "Fifty-four Forty or Fight!" became a national slogan. A magazine editor referred to the "manifest destiny" of the United States to control the North American

48

continent, and the phrase caught on. Newspapers repeated it; politicians repeated it; the people repeated it. Everywhere people talked of America's "manifest destiny" to expand to the west.

Polk won the election. Congress voted to give England the one year's notice required to cancel the Joint Occupation Treaty. After that the United States could proceed to take Oregon—by force if necessary.

At this same time, however, the United States was annexing Texas, which quickly brought on the war with Mexico. President Polk did not want to fight two countries at one time, and England was not anxious to go to war over a country so remote that many considered it worthless.

Compromise is easy when both sides want to avoid trouble. The British foreign minister proposed a treaty that would extend the existing continental border between the United States and Canada along the forty-ninth parallel until it hit the sea at the Strait of Georgia. There it would follow the channel around the south end of Vancouver Island, leaving that island to Canada, and go to the Pacific through the Juan de Fuca Strait. Both countries would have a right to use the channel, and Britain would be given the right of navigation of the Columbia River below the forty-ninth parallel.

On June 15, 1846, the Senate ratified the treaty. Once more the United States had new borders.

One small problem would develop later. Under the terms of the treaty, the border would follow the channel around Vancouver Island, but there were two channels with a cluster of small islands between them. If the boundary followed one channel, these islands belonged to the United States; if it followed the other, they belonged to Canada. This issue was resolved by the arbitration award of 1873, which gave the islands to the United States.

On to California

War With Mexico

IN 1844, when James K. Polk was elected President, his platform was in favor of annexing Texas and also acquiring the Oregon Territory. Polk's platform did not mention New Mexico and California, but the President himself was determined that this area should become part of the United States. One of his first acts as President was to send John Slidell to Mexico with instructions to try to buy the land. The Mexican government refused to sell. At the same time they made it clear that they considered the annexation of Texas, which had already been carried out, an act of war.

At first there was no actual fighting. Americans troops under General Zachary Taylor built a small fort on the north bank of the Rio Grande about where the city of Brownsville now is. Directly across the river, in the town of Matamoros, Mexican troops were stationed in plain view of the Americans. Each afternoon both army bands would play. As one young officer wrote in his diary, "When the sun was declining . . . the female population [of Matamoros] would assemble to see and be seen and listen to the music." The United States band played *"Yankee Doodle* because it made a loud noise, *The Star Spangled Banner* because it waved over us, *Hail Columbia* because it was inspiriting, and the sweetest airs from the operas for the beautiful señoritas." The Mexican band, in its turn, would play "exquisite music."

This blissful state of affairs ended suddenly when General Arista arrived to take command of the Mexican forces. Quickly he sent sixteen hundred cavalry to cross the river above the American fort. These troops met a scouting party of sixty-three Americans and killed or captured nearly all of them. Immedi-

James K. Polk

ately, on April 26, 1846, General Taylor wrote President Polk that "hostilities may now be considered as commenced."

It took the message two weeks to reach Washington. On May 11 Polk told Congress, "Mexico has . . . shed American blood upon American soil. . . . War exists, and . . . exists by the act of Mexico itself."

Polk had not wanted war, but he had wanted California. Now that war was forced on him, he used it to get what he wanted. Quickly he sent word to American ships in the Pacific to capture the California ports. He ordered General Stephen W. Kearny to march from Fort Leavenworth in eastern Kansas all the way to California, and to capture New Mexico on the way. In California he was to cooperate with the navy, conquer the land, and set up an American civil government. At the same time, General Zachary Taylor was ordered to cross the Rio Grande and invade Mexico.

There was some brief but bloody fighting, and then the Mexican troops retreated. The Americans were left in control of northern Mexico, from California to the Gulf. This was all the land that Polk had wanted, and considerably more. The trouble was, the Mexican government still would not agree to peace.

51

General Winfield Scott

To make matters worse for President Polk, the war was not popular in the United States. It was being refered to as "Mr. Polk's War." Many persons claimed it was being fought only to get land for new slave-owning states. They called it "mercenary and base." A young Whig Congressman named Abraham Lincoln said President Polk had begun the war "unnecessarily and unconstitutionally."

The only way to force the Mexicans to surrender, the President decided, was to capture Mexico City itself. To do this, he sent an army under General Winfield Scott by ship to Vera Cruz. From there, little by little, this army fought its way inland.

Along with the army Polk sent a representative of the State Department named Nicholas P. Trist. Trist was empowered to make peace whenever the Mexicans were willing, so long as they agreed to cede California and New Mexico to the United States.

On September 14, 1847, the United States army captured Mexico City, but still no members of the Mexican government would sit down at the conference table with Mr. Trist. One reason was pride. Another reason was a law the Mexican congress had passed. According to it, any person who even talked with the American representative about peace would be considered a traitor.

Finally Polk got tired and ordered Trist home. Trist received the order—and just about the same time he got word that the Mexicans finally were ready to talk.

Now Mr. Trist had a problem. Although he had been ordered home, and his power to make a treaty with Mexico had been revoked, he knew that the President would want the treaty. It would take weeks to get a letter to Washington, and get an answer back. Trist decided to ignore the President's order. He met with the Mexican representatives, and on February 2, 1848, they signed the Treaty of Guadalupe Hidalgo.

Once more a new border was set. It ran from the Gulf up the middle of the Rio Grande River "to a point where it strikes the southern boundary of New Mexico." This was the Mexican province of New Mexico, not the state as it is now. The southern boundary was to be as shown on a map drawn a short time before by a man named J. Disturnell. From here the line followed the border of New Mexico to the Gila River. It followed the Gila to the Colorado River, and from there ran in a straight line along the thirty-second parallel to the Pacific.

1848. The Mexican Border.

For this new territory, which included all of present-day California and Nevada, and parts of Utah, Arizona, and New Mexico, the United States agreed to pay $15,000,000. A party of engineers, some from the United States and some from Mexico, would survey this new border and mark it.

53

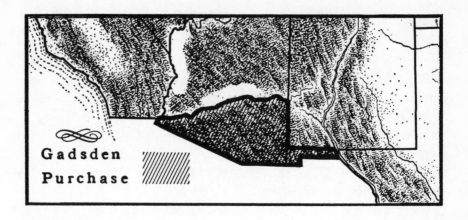

The Gadsden Purchase

UNDER THE Treaty of Guadalupe Hidalgo, which set a new boundary between the United States and Mexico, commissioners from both nations were to meet and mark the new border. They agreed on the western end of the line without trouble. But when it came to deciding just where the Rio Grande met the border of the Mexican state of New Mexico, things became confused.

According to the treaty, this point was to be decided by the Disturnell Map. But one of the first things the commissioners discovered was that the town of El Paso was actually more than sixty miles south of where the map showed it. Then it turned out that the river itself was nearly one hundred and forty miles east of where it was on the map.

What now? Should they mark the border according to the latitude and longitude as shown on the Disturnell Map? Or should they mark it according to the map's location of the town and river? Quite naturally the United States commissioners wanted the most they could get, and the Mexicans wanted to lose the least possible.

After long argument, the commissioners agreed on everything except a strip of land about thirty miles deep and almost two hundred miles long. Not more than three thousand persons lived in this whole area, some of them Mexicans, some Americans. The land itself was poor, but there was one thing that made it of great importance—it offered what many engineers thought was the very best route for a railroad to the Pacific.

This was at a time in American history when the whole country was railroad crazy. Gold had just been discovered in California. Pioneers were pouring westward into Oregon. The United States needed a railroad to tie the east and west coasts together. The south side of the Gila River was really a much better location for a railroad than the north side.

The argument over who owned the land went on for several years, until it began to look as if once more the United States and Mexico might go to war.

Finally, in 1853, the matter was settled at the conference table. James Gadsden of Charlestown, South Carolina, was the American representative. The agreement that resulted was known as the Gadsden Treaty, signed December 30, 1853. Under it the United States agreed to pay Mexico $15,000,000 and to assume responsibility for the claims that some Americans had made against the Mexican government. In return, in what is called the Gadsden Purchase, Mexico sold the United States some 45,535 square miles south of the Gila River. It was the land that today forms the southwestern corner of New Mexico and all of southern Arizona.

With it, except for very minor changes, the land that today forms the forty-eight states of the United States mainland had taken its final shape.

Alaska

A Forgotten Land

VITUS BERING was a squat, slow-speaking Danish explorer employed by the Czar of Russia. In July, 1741, he was sailing his ship through unknown, fog-shrouded waters of the North Pacific when suddenly a rift opened in the clouds ahead of him. Looking up, he saw the tremendous volcano now called St. Elias. He had discovered the land now named Alaska.

Bering, who was sick with scurvy, did not live to return to Russia, but those of his men who did return took with them a number of sea-otter furs. These they sold for fantastic prices. Before long Russian fur hunters were racing to the Aleutian Islands and on to Alaska, where they established a few settlements.

Word of the otter furs spread around the world. American and British trappers began to compete with the Russians. To keep them out of the area, the Russian Czar, in 1821, made a flat claim to all the land north of the fifty-first parallel. He also decreed the Pacific Ocean north of this line closed to merchant ships of other nations.

The fifty-first parallel lay well within what was called Oregon Territory, and both the American and British governments reacted vigorously. In 1823, when President James Monroe issued the Monroe Doctrine warning other countries not to establish new colonies in America, he was looking straight at Russia. The English backed him up.

Russia did not want war with two countries at once. In 1824 and 1825, she made treaties with the United States and Britain which for the first time set a definite southern boundary for Russian-owned Alaska. This boundary was set at 54° 40'.

Strange as it may now seem, the next change in Alaskan ownership would be partly the result of the United States Civil War.

William Seward

During that war both England and France were friendly to the South, while Russian sympathy was with the North. This helped create a warm friendship between the North and Russia.

By this time the Alaskan fur trade was almost gone. Russia had not developed Alaska, and now the country was costing her money. She was anxious to sell, and William Seward, the United States Secretary of State, was anxious to buy. Seward believed in an expanding America. On March 30, 1867, he signed a treaty to buy Alaska for $7,200,000.

Although Seward was anxious to buy Alaska, a great many other Americans were not. Some of them called it "Seward's Folly," "Seward's Icebox" and a "Polar-Bear Garden." One congressman announced that "every foot of the soil of Alaska is frozen from five to six feet deep." It was largely because of American friendship for Russia that the Senate finally approved the treaty.

Having bought Alaska, the American government promptly forgot it. For a long time no government of any kind was established there. Land was not opened to settlers as it had been on other frontiers, nor could it be bought or sold legally since there was no place to register a deed. There were no courts to punish crime. There was not even any legal way to be married.

It was because of this treatment that one Alaskan poet wrote about his country's attitude toward the United States:

> Sitting on my greatest glacier
>   with my feet in Bering Sea,
> I am thinking cold and lonely
>   of the way you've treated me. . .
>
> When you took me, young and trusting,
>   from the growling Russian Bear,
> Loud you swore before the nation
>   I should have the eagle's care.
> Never yet has wing of eagle
>   cast a shadow on my peaks,
> But I've watched the flight of buzzards,
>   and I've felt their busy beaks.

Alaska Is Rediscovered

IT WAS the discovery of gold in 1880 that first made the United States aware of its northern possession, and brought some shadow of government. Even so, it was not until 1912 that Alaska was given full territorial government such as had been given to other territories almost immediately. Once that government was established, however, the forty-eight states once more forgot the vast land to the north.

When World War II began, Alaska was suddenly rediscovered. In an age of intercontinental airplanes, Alaska was no longer remote. It was, in fact, almost midway between the United States and Asia. Japan lay just south of the Aleutians and soon the Japanese were moving into these islands, heading toward Alaska and easy bombing range of American cities.

Immediately United States troops poured into Alaska. Many discovered, to their surprise, that Alaska was not the frozen wilderness they had believed it to be. They found in many places that the climate was very pleasant and the soil so rich that crops seemed to spring from the ground. Many soldiers and sailors liked what they found, and stayed in Alaska after the war. The whole nation became Alaska-conscious.

And so on January 3, 1959, Alaska became the forty-ninth and largest state in the Union—twice the size of Texas, with a single glacier as big as Rhode Island, and a coastline so long it would more than circle the globe.

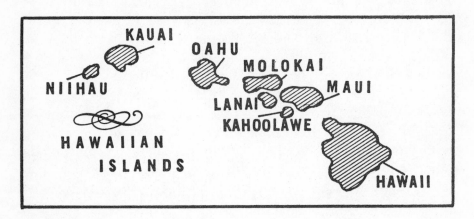

Hawaii

Paradise in the Pacific

IN THE YEAR 1778, an English explorer named Captain James Cook, was on his way to explore the northwest coast of America when he came upon an incredibly beautiful group of islands peopled by a brown-skinned, handsome, and friendly people. Cook named these islands the Sandwich Islands, after a British nobleman, the Earl of Sandwich. Today they are called the Hawaiian Islands.

After Cook's voyage, English and American merchants began to send ships to the Pacific Northwest for furs. This fur trade was a kind of three-cornered business. The furs were collected along the coast of America, then taken to China for sale, where they brought fantastic prices. In turn, this money was invested in spices and silks, which were sold in England and America for still more profit.

It was a very long voyage across the Pacific, and the Hawaiian Islands offered a convenient stopover. There ships could take on fresh water, fresh meat, and fruits. The climate was wonderful, the scenery beautiful, and the people friendly. More than one sailor, enchanted by these islands, decided he had voyaged far enough and remained behind when his ship sailed away.

At this time the islands were ruled by a number of native kings, sometimes two or more on the same island. Then came the greatest of all the Hawaiian kings, Kamehameha I. Starting with the biggest island of the group, he conquered most of the others one by one. Those he did not conquer he persuaded to join him. By about 1810 Kamehameha ruled all the islands.

A Boy Named Henry

DURING these wars of conquest, the parents of a Hawaiian boy named Henry Obookiah were killed fighting on the losing side. Young Henry then joined the crew of an American ship visiting Hawaii and eventually wound up in Boston. Here one day a preacher named E. W. Dwight found him sitting cold and miserable on the steps of Yale University. The Reverend Dwight took Henry home with him. They talked about Hawaii and Henry told the preacher about the Hawaiian religion. It was a primitive religion with a great many taboos and terrible punishments for breaking them. Now Henry was interested in the

Kamehameha II

white man's religion. Many of his people, he thought, would **be** equally interested. The Reverend Dwight was soon hard at work looking for missionaries to go to Hawaii.

As a result, a shipload of American missionaries arrived in Hawaii in 1820. The first thing they learned was that Kamehameha I was dead. The new king, Kamehameha II, had abolished the old taboos. This left the islands with no enforced religion at all. When the missionaries started teaching Christianity, many of the islanders quickly accepted it.

61

Meanwhile, more and more ships were visiting the islands, and more and more countries becoming interested in them. England, France, Russia, and the United States all considered claiming them. Perhaps it was because so many countries were concerned that no one nation did grab the islands by force.

The Americans

A NUMBER of Americans came to the islands and went into business. Land was cheap; sugarcane, pineapples, and bananas grew rapidly in the rich soil. There was good grazing for cattle. The sons of the early missionaries grew up in Hawaii; many of them went into business there and became wealthy.

In 1872 King Kamehameha V died without an heir. The Hawaiians, who were learning many things from their white visitors, decided to elect the new king by vote. Already they had an elected legislature that helped the king rule. The Hawaiian people were moving rapidly toward a form of democracy.

Many of the American settlers, however, were anxious to be annexed by the United States. With most of them this was not so much a matter of patriotism as it was of business. If Hawaii belonged to the United States, those who lived there could ship their goods into the U.S. without paying a tariff, and so increase their profits. Even when one of the Hawaiian kings visited America and signed a treaty that permitted Hawaiian goods to enter the country free, many of the settlers were not satisfied. Under United States law, sugar produced in the United States or its possessions brought a bonus price. The men who owned the sugarcane fields in Hawaii wanted this bonus along with other financial benefits that would be theirs if Hawaii were part of the United States.

Grover Cleveland

In 1893 these men overthrew the native Hawaiian government. They established what was called the Republic of Hawaii and asked to be annexed by the United States.

Many persons in the United States wanted to annex Hawaii, but there were also many who thought that to take over the islands against the wishes of most of the native people was altogether wrong. Grover Cleveland, the newly elected President, agreed with this. To take the islands in this way, he said, "is not expedient, because it is not just."

Cleveland's pronouncement temporarily stopped the move for annexation, and for a few years the Hawaiian Islands continued as an independent republic. Then, in 1897, William McKinley became President. Quickly the men who ruled Hawaii sent another petition for annexation. While it was being considered, the United States became involved in the Spanish-American War. American ships attacking the Spanish-owned Philippines needed a base in the Pacific, and Pearl Harbor, Hawaii, was one of the finest harbors in the world.

Hawaii Joins the Union

SWIFTLY Congress voted to annex the islands. On July 7, 1898, President McKinley signed the bill. Hawaii became an American territory.

Because of the great naval base at Pearl Harbor, the United States did not forget its island possession as it had forgotten Alaska. Also, Hawaii's climate and the amazing beauty of its landscape drew a steady stream of tourists. Even so, many United States congressmen were not anxious to take the islands as a state in the Union. They seemed too remote, too different from the forty-eight states on the mainland. A great many Japanese and Chinese had immigrated to the islands, and had intermarried with the Hawaiians, the Americans, and one another. On the mainland many persons wondered if these people, with their mixed background, could be loyal Americans.

World War II brought the answer. Not a single act of sabotage was committed by the islanders. More than 40,000 of the island men joined the armed forces and served with great valor around the world. One battalion made up of Hawaiians of Japanese ancestry became the most decorated unit in the army. Obviously, Hawaii was now American.

On August 21, 1959, Hawaii became the fiftieth state in the Union. The borders of the United States of America were complete as they now stand.

Index